How to Convert Your Published Book into an Audio Book.

Expand your audience and increase your royalties!

Lynda D. Brown

ISBN: 978-0-9850913-7-8

DEDICATION

This Book is dedicated to each and every self published author that took the great leap of faith and published their own books!

CONTENTS

INTRODUCTION

There's a huge demand for your book! As an independent publisher, I try to stay abreast of everything new in self publishing, so imagine my surprise when I discovered I was missing out on a very important audience and potential income base. While putting together my notes on Amazon and Kindle Direct Publishing for a workshop that I'm doing, I discovered that Amazon had purchased Audible.com. Audible is known for its audio books. Intrigued, I dug a little further and discovered that Create Space and Kindle Direct publishers can now convert their published titles into audio books!

How big is the market and demand? In 2009 over 100,000 self published titles were published on Amazon. Only 5000 of those books were also available as an audio book or download. That's a huge market share that we're losing money on if we're not a part of this very lucrative market. When my first book came out, a fan asked if it was available in audio. She explained to me that her employer allows her to listen to audio books while working, so this is her preferred format. Having researched this field before, I knew that publishing an audio book was beyond my financial capabilities, so I was really blown away when I realized I could produce my books into audio format with a professional narrator, and sell it on Audible.com, Apple's iTunes store and Amazon.com, with no up front cost!!!

In this step-by-step guide, I'm going to show you how to:

- ⟑ Create a compelling title profile
- ⟑ Explain what a 'producer' is and how you can get one.
- ⟑ Audition narrators for your book
- ⟑ Produce your book with no out of pocket expenses!
- ⟑ Create your book cover jacket for your audio book
- ⟑ Approve the final product
- ⟑ Sell your audio books on Audible.com, iTunes.com and Amazon.com
- ⟑ Earn extra royalties on your audio book!

Once you get the hang of this, you'll want to convert all of your published works into audio books so your new audience will be aware of all your books.

STEP ONE: GETTING STARTED

This is where all the magic begins.......To get started, log onto this website: https://www.acx.com/

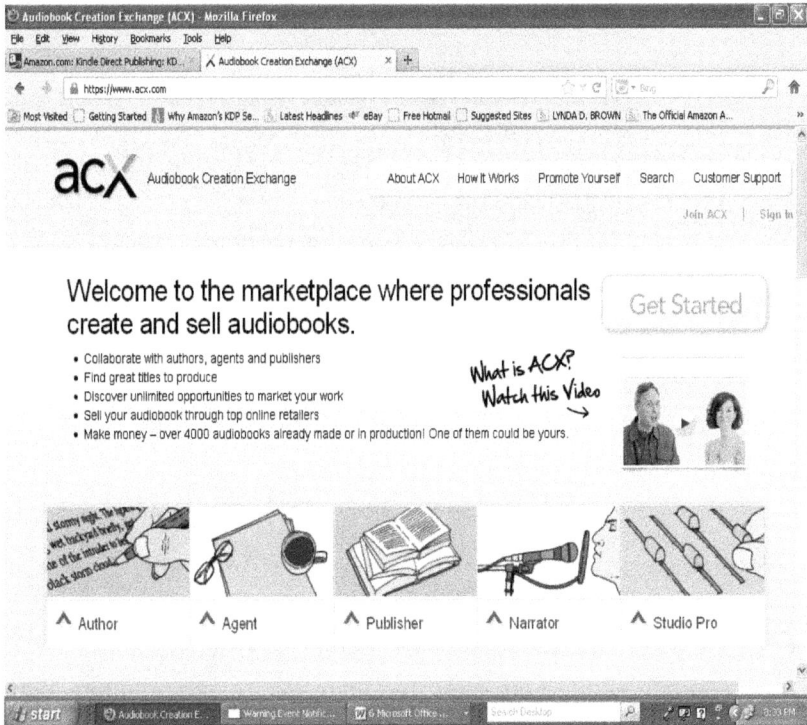

Click on Join ACX in the upper right hand corner. It should take you to this screen:

Yes, that's right, to join ACX, you only need to be a member of Amazon.com!! Make sure you log in with your Amazon Kindle Direct Publishing account information.

STEP TWO: CREATE YOUR TITLE PROFILE

Once you log in Click on Authors. The page should look like this:

Scroll down and click on *Find your book on ACX and claim it!*

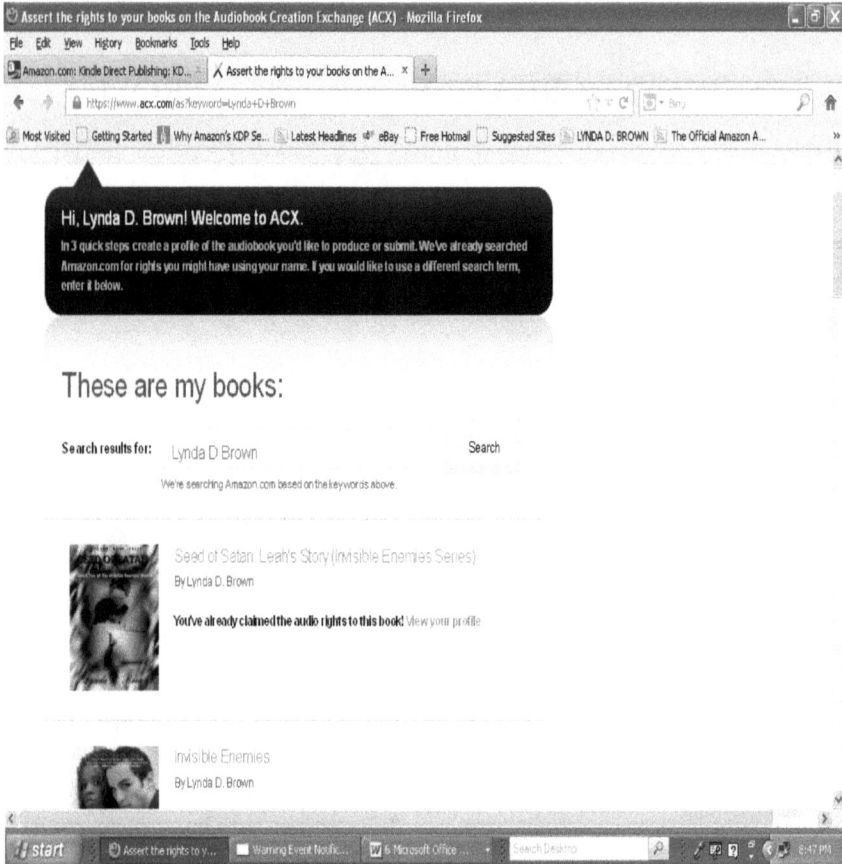

This link will find your titles on Amazon. If you published with Author House, Strategic Book Publishing Group, Xlibris, etc…it's very important for you to read your contract and make sure you still own the audio rights to your book!

When you locate your book, click on it. Your book description from Amazon will appear in the about my book section. Do not edit this. You want it to look the same as your Amazon page.

Next, fill out the Copyright information just as it appears in your book:

This is very easy and self explanatory.

Describe the ideal narrator's voice:

This section is very important, so please take some time and think about how you want the person narrating your book to sound. Does it sound better with a male or female? Accent or not? Always remember you can edit this section at any time. There's also a box for extra comments. Read that information carefully for more directions to your narrator.

Audition Script:

You can upload a 'script' of your book to your profile, so narrators can read from your book and return for you to listen. I use my book's synopses as the audition script. Whatever you decided to use, make sure it's brief.

For payment and distribution information, I'm going to refer you to the ACX website. If you are a KDP and or Create Space Author, this information will be very familiar.

This section tells ACX how you want to get paid and how you would like to distribute your audio books.

https://www.acx.com/help/payments/200474570

STEP THREE: FIND A PRODUCER OR PRODUCE YOUR AUDIO BOOK YOURSELF

Once you have your title profile filled out, the next step is to find a narrator or 'producer' to narrate and produce your audio book. Please don't just sit idly by and wait for someone to find your book, I actively sought out 'producers' for my Invisible Enemies Series, and after listening to a couple of different voices, I found a woman I was interested in, sent her a message via ACX and asked her to audition. She did and within 48 hours I had a contract with her to do not one, but both my supernatural thrillers and she agreed to do it with out any upfront money, but a 50/50 royalty split!

To me it was a win-win situation. I found a professional narrator, who would do the narration and produce the audio book and upload it to ACX upon completion!

Another great feature using this system is ACX is responsible for making all payments to my producer! I don't have to be bothered with bookkeeping.

ACX also gives you the option to narrate your book yourself! To find out more about that option, you can find it here: https://www.acx.com/help/authors-as-narrators/200626860

For those of you that would rather keep all the royalties, you can also arrange a 'pay for production' deal, where you would pay the producer an agreed upon 'fee per finished hour.' I'm currently using this option for my new non fiction book and it's been getting a lot of attention from producers and studios!

STEP FOUR: REVIEW AUDITIONS

Once your profile has been set up and you've decided what type of voice you'd like to narrate your book, the next thing you want to do is began auditioning producers.

Search for Narrators by clicking on search and the drop down will list Narrators for hire and Titles accepting auditions. (See below):

If you find someone you like, send them a message via the ACX website:

The producer will record the audition and send it back to you for your review. *Listen carefully.* If the voice and your book are a match, you're on your way to securing a contract to get your book produced. If the narrator's voice just doesn't work for your project, you can politely decline via the system. It's all very professional. Remain *diligent* until you find the right fit.

STEP FIVE: MAKE A DEAL WITH A PRODUCER

You've found the ideal producer and now you'd like to make them an offer to produce your audio book. You have two things to consider:

1) Royalty Share payment – No upfront payments. You can do a 50/50 royalty split or

2) Fee-Per-Production Hour- You can pay your producer a set fee per production hour rate, let him or her produce the audio book and you keep 100% royalties.

I currently have three projects in the works, two are for royalty share splits and one is a fee per production hour rate, and I will collect all my royalties for this project.

Since this section deals with contracts, please read this for yourself. Here's the link for this information on the ACX website: https://www.acx.com/help/offers/200492840

Once you've secured a contract with the producer of your choice, the next step is to upload a cover for your new audio book!

STEP SIX: UPLOADING YOUR AUDIO BOOK COVER

Did you notice that your book cover file didn't transfer over with the description of your book on Amazon? Unfortunately, you won't be able to use the same jpeg image size, but you can still use the same book cover as your print or eBook.

Audio book covers are square, and eBook and print covers are more rectangular. Your new audio book cover needs to be 1200x1200 pixels. I found a quick and easy way to do this by using a jpeg image resizer that I found: http://images.my-addr.com/resize_jpg_online_tool-free_jpeg_resizer_for_web.php

Just log onto the site and upload your book cover file and increase the width to 1200 and the height to 1200 and that's all to it!

STEP SEVEN: APPROVAL OF FINAL PRODUCT

The audio book production process will last anywhere between 3-8 weeks depending on the length of your book. Your producer should send you via the ACX website, the first 15 minutes of him or her narrating your book. Take your time and listen to the narrator's voice, diction and accent. You also want to pay attention to the quality of the recording, editing and if you need to, feel free to offer the producer suggestions to make the book really flow.

If you aren't satisfied with the project, ask the producer to make some changes. They can make up to two rounds of corrections or edits.

Once you're satisfied with the final product, the producer will upload the completed file to the ACX website and will be paid if they had a fee per production hour arrangement.

Producers with a royalty sharing arrangement will upload the final product to the ACX website and will collect 50% of the royalty payments for the life of the audio book!

Authors who are not happy with the project after two editorial rounds can cancel the project; however a 'kill fee' may apply. Please see the ***ACX Audiobook Production Standard Terms:*** https://www.acx.com/help/production-standard-terms/200485540

STEP EIGHT: DISTRIBUTE YOUR AUDIO BOOK ON AUDIBLE.COM, AMAZON.COM AND ITUNES.COM

ACX allows authors an opportunity to distribute their books exclusively or non-exclusively on ACX. If you choose to grant ACX exclusive distribution rights to your audiobook, they will oversee distribution of your book to the three major audiobook distributors, Audible.com, Amazon.com and Apple's iTune.com stores. If you prefer to grant ACX non-exclusive distribution rights, then you can distribute your audio book through additional channels, however, any channels outside of ACX will have to be arranged by the author, not ACX.

I do want to remind authors that if you choose to distribute exclusively through ACX, your royalty rate is higher! For more information, click on the link below:
https://www.acx.com/help/distribution/200474580

STEP NINE: HOW TO EARN *MORE* ROYALTIES ON YOUR AUDIO BOOKS!

How much will my audio book sell for in the stores? This is a great question and I wanted to make sure you could find it here without having to search all over the website.

The regular price on Audible.com for the product is generally priced based on its length, as follows:

- ⚔ under 3 hours: under $10
- ⚔ 3 – 5 hours: $10 - $20
- ⚔ 5 – 10 hours: $15 - $25
- ⚔ 10 – 20 hours: $20 - $30
- ⚔ over 20 hours: $25 – 35

Authors will receive a monthly royalty statement and payment from Audible. Payments are calculated per book, so the more books you sell, the more money you earn!

But wait.....ACX has even more ways for authors to make money with audiobooks. Depending on the distribution rights, and the arrangement you make with producers, authors can receive escalating monthly royalty fees of up to 90%!

If you're an author working under a pay for fee production deal, ACX will pay you an extra $25 every time your audio book is one of the three audiobooks purchased by an AudibleListener member on Audible.com! If you're an author working under a royalty share deal, you'll share the $25 with your producer for a total of $12.50 each per book! For more information about payments view: https://www.acx.com/help/payments/200474570

Don't forget to fill out your IRS W-9 form for tax purposes. You'll find the form by clicking on the link above.

STEP TEN: PROMOTE YOUR AUDIO BOOK

Of course you want to use social media to promote your audio book just like you promote your print or eBook. ACX has a great section on using social media to promote your book so here's the link to this section of the website:

https://www.acx.com/help/promote-yourself/200485310

All the favorites are here and some new ones:

Facebook

Twitter

LinkedIn

YouTube

Google+

Pinterest

Podcasting

Email blast

How can I take advantage of the new Kindle and Audible features Whispersync for Voice and Immersion Reading to reach more readers in more ways?

If your book has a Kindle book version, you can use ACX to produce a digital audiobook version of your book, and to make your book eligible for the new Whispersync for Voice functionality which allows customers to switch seamlessly between reading a Kindle book and listening to the corresponding, professionally narrated audiobook across devices without losing their place. Audiobooks will also be eligible for the new Immersion Reading feature, which allows customers with the new Kindle Fire and Kindle Fire HD devices to listen to a professionally narrated audiobook from Audible as the text of the corresponding eBook is highlighted on the screen. When customers buy your Kindle book, they will be able to purchase your Whispersync for Voice-ready Audible audiobook at a special limited time discounted price.

Thank you for purchasing this eBook. I hope the information in here will assist you in setting up your ACX account and finding the right producers to help you create your audiobooks.

If you need further information contact ACX.com or email me at: Spokenwordpress2010@gmail.com

Lynda Brown
Spoken Word Press Publishing

www.ingramcontent.com/pod-product-compliance
Lightning Source LLC
Chambersburg PA
CBHW070113070426
42448CB00038B/2663